Geo's Adventure Colouring Book

Explore Saint Lucia

Historic Sites
Culture and Festivals
Important People

by Sadia W Verneuil

ISBN 978-1-387-84580-4

Editing by Kate Cornibert
Cover design by Sadia Wendy Verneuil
Illustrations by Sadia Wendy Verneuil

Printed in and bound in the United States of America by Lulu.com

Published by Miss-Vee Art Studio
Castries,
Saint Lucia
msverneuil@gmail.com

Visit www.miss-vee.com/colllections/educational-resources

This book belongs to:

Will

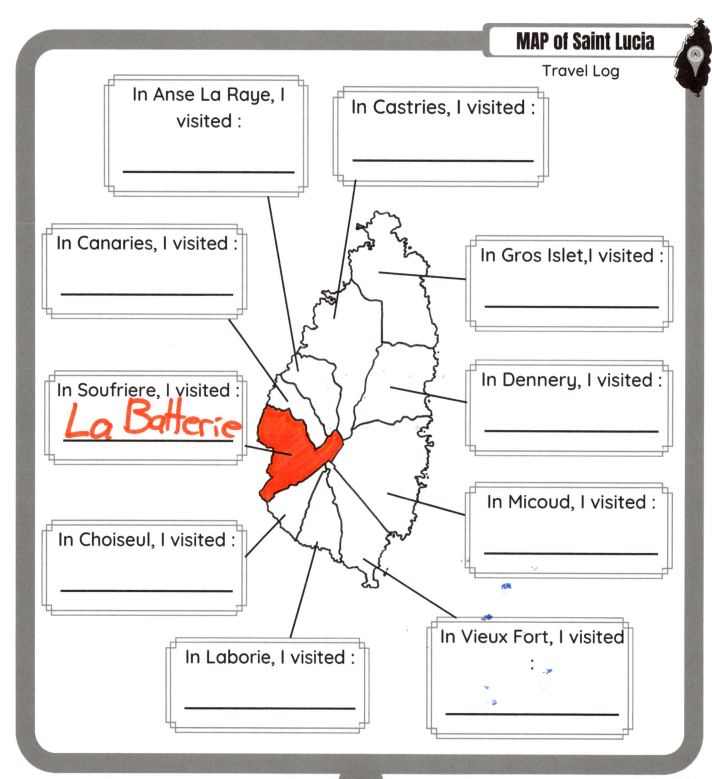

In Anse La Raye, I visited :

_____

In Castries, I visited :

_____

In Canaries, I visited :

_____

In Gros Islet, I visited :

_____

In Soufriere, I visited :

La Batterie

In Dennery, I visited :

_____

In Choiseul, I visited :

_____

In Micoud, I visited :

_____

In Laborie, I visited :

_____

In Vieux Fort, I visited :

_____

All About My Field Trip to:

Before...

I wonder if...

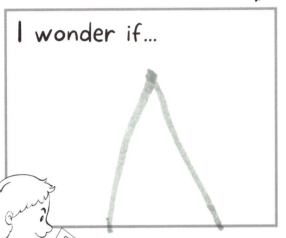

I can't wait to see...

After...

I saw...

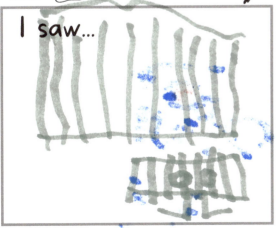

I learned about...

All About My Field Trip to:

Before...

I wonder if...

I can't wait to see...

After...

I saw...

I learned about...

All About My Field Trip to:

Before...

I wonder if...

I can't wait to see...

After...

I saw...

I learned about...

All About My Field Trip to:

Before...

I wonder if...

I can't wait to see...

After...

I saw...

I learned about...

All About My Field Trip to: _____

Before...

I wonder if...	I can't wait to see...

After...

I saw...	I learned about...

All About My Field Trip to:

Before...

| I wonder if... | I can't wait to see... |

After...

| I saw... | I learned about... |

All About My Field Trip to:

Before...

I wonder if...	I can't wait to see...

After...

I saw...	I learned about...

All About My Field Trip to:

Before...

I wonder if...	I can't wait to see...

After...

I saw...	I learned about...

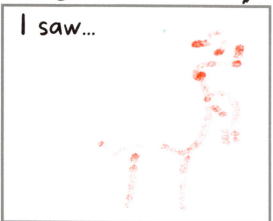

All About My Field Trip to:

Before...

I wonder if...

I can't wait to see...

After...

I saw...

I learned about...

All About My Field Trip to:

Before...

I wonder if...	I can't wait to see...

After...

I saw...	I learned about...

A	N	S	E	L	A	R	A	Y	E
G	C	A	N	A	R	I	E	S	Q
H	R	S	J	K	M	N	O	L	P
C	H	O	I	S	E	U	L	A	V
W	X	U	S	Y	C	O	P	B	I
D	P	F	Z	I	A	Q	R	O	E
E	Q	R	M	W	S	U	T	R	U
N	R	I	I	X	T	L	V	I	X
N	S	E	C	Y	R	D	E	E	F
E	T	R	O	Z	I	F	H	T	O
R	U	E	U	V	E	G	J	K	R
Y	N	M	D	L	S	C	B	A	T

SOUFRIERE
CHOISEUL
LABORIE
VIEUX FORT
MICOUD
GROS ISLET
CASTRIES
ANSE LA RAYE
CANARIES
DENNERY

17

Historical Sites

The Pitons are a World Heritage Site. Petit Piton is in Soufriere. It is 743 m (2,438 ft) high. Gros Piton is in Choiseul. It is 798.25 m (2,618.9 ft) high. The Pitons were created less than a million years ago by volcanic activity which still can be witnessed at the Sulphur Springs volcano located nearby. Amerindians considered the mountains to have mystical powers and early European explorers noted their unique and splendid beauty.

The Minor Basilica of the Immaculate Conception in Castries is the largest Catholic church in the Region. It was given the honorary status of a Minor Basilica on May 11, 1999 as part of the centenary celebrations.

The interior is decorated with a mural by St. Lucian artist, Sir Dunstan St. Omer.

The Moule- a – Chique Lighthouse was built in 1912 and is said to be the world's second highest lighthouse. Its actual height is 740 feet above sea level. It is located in Vieux-Fort.

The Maria Islands—Maria Major and Maria Minor—are a protected wildlife reserve, accessible via a boat ride from Pointe Sable, Vieux-Fort. Maria Major is the habitat of some native reptile species, including the Saint Lucia Whiptail Lizard and the Racer, a nonvenomous grass snake. The islet has a variety of unusual tropical flora and fauna and its waters are rich with coral reefs. The reserve is a nesting ground for migratory birds that flock there from Africa.

Balenbouche was first established as a sugar and rum-producing Caribbean plantation in the 1740's. African slaves were brought to work the plantations. Between 1859 and 1893, Balenbouche Estate was one of the few plantations in the South to use Indentured Laborers from East India to work on the plantation.

Pigeon Island was once just an island, until it was later connected to the northern portion of Saint Lucia in 1971, via a causeway. Pigeon Island was first occupied by the Amerindians, mainly Caribs. The island was later occupied by pirates. Forts were built in the area and operated by both the French and the British . The British, during initial rule over the island, used a heavily fortified Pigeon Island to spy on the French in nearby Martinique.

Remnants of old sugar mills can be found in some parts of the island, such as in the community of Morne Sion, Choiseul.

Sugarcane was first introduced into St.Lucia in 1764 and the first sugar plantation was started near Vieux-Fort in 1765.

By 1789, there were 43 estates growing sugarcane on the island. During this period, thousands of slaves were brought into St.Lucia from West Africa to work on these plantations. In 1777, the population of St.Lucia was 19,000. Of these, 16,000 were slaves.

Almost all the estates had its own mill. Some were operated by cattle, some by wind and others by steam. These mills were used to drive the machinery that crushed the sugarcane to get the juice that made the sugar. By 1843, there were 803 sugar estates in St.Lucia.

The Diamond Waterfalls flow off the Sulphur Springs. Natural minerals found in the area include, Kaolinite and Quartz and smaller quantities of Gypsum, Alunite, Pyrite and Geothite. In 1784, the Baron de Laborie, the then Governor of St. Lucia, sent samples of the mineral water to Paris to be analyzed by the "Medicine du Roi". The waters from the Diamond Springs were found to have the same properties as the famous Aix-les-Bains in France and Aix-la-Chapelle or Aachen in Germany. Bathing in these therapeutic waters has been recommended for persons who suffer from chronic rheumatism, respiratory complaints and ulcers, an opinion supported by John Davy M.D., the Inspector General of military hospitals in the West Indies, circa 1850. Dr. Davy carried out a more detailed analysis in 1854, elaborating on the mineral content of these "healing" waters.

The Sulphur Springs Park is located in the town of Soufriere. It is known as, "The World's Only Drive-In Volcano".

At Sulphur Springs Park, you are in the middle of a dormant volcano and at the site of the last recorded eruption in 1766.The park's main attraction is its sulphur springs - a collection of boiling springs and fumeroles that is seated 305 metres above sea level, between the Rabot Ridge and Terre Blanche. The springs, from which the area gets its name, Sulphur Springs, occur at the intersection of two fault lines which traverse the centre of a large steep sided volcanic depression, called "Qualibou" caldera. This caldera is about 32,000 to 39,000 years old. Between 1974 to 1988, several attempts were made to harness the energy of the area. As a result, 9 exploratory wells were drilled to various depths in and around the area to explore the possibility of geothermal energy.

The Government House, which serves as the official residence of the Governor General, is one of the main historical sites of Saint Lucia, dating back to 1895. Situated at Morne Fortune on the outskirts of the city of Castries, the building reflects the period of Victorian architecture and is a popular attraction for persons interested in the history of Saint Lucia.

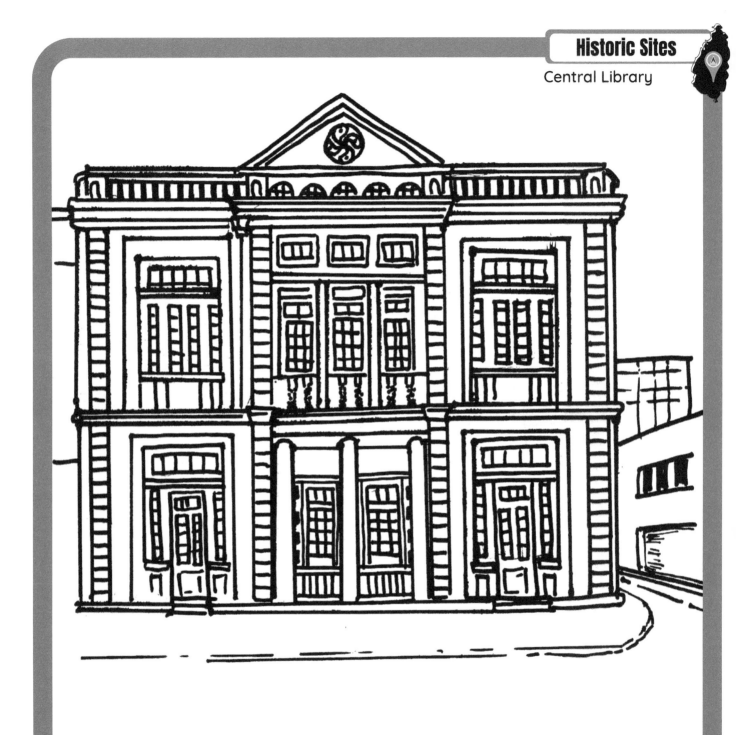

Andrew Carnegie Public Library, also known as, the Central Library, is located on Bourbon Street, next to the Derek Walcott Square in Castries.

The library cornerstone was laid on May 15, 1923. It was completed in June 1924 and was called the Carnegie Free Library. The first building escaped the 1927 Castries fire, but the 1948 Castries fire gutted the enitre structure, destroying over 20,000 books in the process. After the blaze, the library was rebuilt using the same old walls.

The Grace Church is one of the first Anglican churches built in Saint Lucia. It is significant because it was built in no small part, by the newly freed slaves. The Anglican Church also gifted Saint Lucia with two holidays - Whit Monday and Thanksgiving. There is a school nearby, towards the back of the church. This was the first school built in St Lucia, immediately after the Emancipation.

WELCOME TO RIVER DOREE
† GRACE CHURCH †
WAS BUILT IN 1846 BY THE
ALEXANDER FAMILY OF
SCOTLAND. THE FAMILY
REMAINS AND THOSE AFRICAN
PRINCE-PRINCE JOHN LIE IN THE
CEMETRY ACROSS THE ROAD

THE SCHOOL WAS THE FIRST
TO BE BUILT AFTER
EMANCIPATION IN 1834

Signage of the Anglican Church, named Grace
Church, in River Doree, Choiseul.

Culture and Festivals

Saint Lucia celebrates its independence on February 22 of every year. Many activities are organised, leading up to that day. The Independence Day parade is one of the common highlights of these celebrations. The National Flag can be seen hoisted at many locations. The colours blue, yellow, black and white are used in decorations on poles, sidewalks and buildings.

The British first took control of the island in 1663, and control of the island changed 14 times, being ruled seven times by the French and seven times by the British. The change in ownership finally stopped with the British gaining control in 1814 as part of the Treaty of Paris, which ended the Napoleonic Wars with Saint Lucia becoming a part of the British Windward Islands colony.

In 1958, Saint Lucia joined the West Indies Federation when the Island's colony was dissolved. In 1967, Saint Lucia became a self-governing island as one of the six members of the West Indies Associated States.

On February 22nd 1979, Saint Lucia gained full independence under Sir John Compton of the conservative United Workers Party (UWP). Sir John later served as Prime Minister.

The National Flowers of Saint Lucia are the Rose and the Marguerite flowers. They are the symbols of the two flower societies of Saint Lucia.

Saint Lucia has two flower festivals- The La Woz and the La Magwit. La Woz, creole for "The Rose", is one of the two historic cultural societies of Saint Lucia. It is also the name of the society's festival, held every August 30. The other societé is La Magwit, creole for "The Marguerite", which holds its festival annually on October 17.

The National Tree of Saint Lucia is the Calabash Tree.

The National Plant of Saint Lucia is the Bamboo.

Bamboo bursting is usually done during the creole celebrations leading up to Christmas.

Saint Lucia's National Dish is Green fig and Saltfish. Green fig refers to green banana.

Blue - 1
Red - 2
Green-3
Gray - 4
Brown- 5
Yellow- 6

The National Bird of Saint Lucia is the Amazona Versicolor. It is also called the Jacquot.

Blue - 1   Yellow-2   Black-3   White-4

The National Flag of Saint Lucia was designed by
Sir Dunstan St.Omer.
Blue represents the sea and the sky.
Black represents the black people.
White represents the white people.
Yellow represents the sunshine and prosperity.
The triangles represent the pitons.

The Wob Dwiyet is Saint Lucia's National Dress. The Madras, also called the Jupe, was originally derived from the Wob Dwiyet. It is commonly worn during cultural celebrations and is recognised as a national attire.

The Masquerade is a Christmas tradition. The slaves used the European Christmas tradition to tell the story of the evil of slavery. Masquerade season begins on December 13 in Saint Lucia.

THE·LAND   THE·LIGHT

THE·PEOPLE

Another of Saint Lucia's National Symbols -
The Coat of Arms.

The Coat of Arms of Saint Lucia was designed by Sydney Bagshaw in 1967. The Coat of Arms is made of a blue shield with a stool, two roses and two fleur de lis. The shield is supported by two Saint Lucian parrots. Beneath the shield is the national motto, whereas, above is a torch and an ornament.

The symbolism of the elements are:

- Tudor Rose – England
- Fleur de lis – France
- Stool – Africa
- Torch – Beacon to light the path
- Saint Lucia Parrot – Amazona Versicolor, the National Bird
- Motto: "The Land, The People, The Light"

Did you know?...

Important People

Sir Derek Walcott

Sir Derek Alton Walcott was a Saint Lucian poet and playwright. He received the 1992 Nobel Prize in Literature. He was born January 23, 1930. He died March 17, 2017.

Sir Arthur Lewis

Sir William Arthur Lewis was a Saint Lucian economist. In 1979, he was awarded the Nobel Memorial Prize in Economic Sciences. He was born January 23, 1915. He died June 15, 1991.

Alfred Nobel was an inventor, entrepreneur, scientist and businessman who also wrote poetry and drama. He invented dynamite! His varied interests are reflected in the prize he established and which he lay the foundation for in 1895, when he wrote his last will. Much of his wealth was left to the establishment of the prize.

Since 1901, the Nobel Prize has been honoring men and women from around the world for outstanding achievements in physics, chemistry, physiology or medicine, literature and for work in peace. Additionally, there is an economics prize awarded at the Nobel ceremony .

The announcement of winners comes a full year after the process starts. The Nobel Committee invites more than 6,000 individuals to submit names for consideration. The committee then screens nominations and gets a working list. By Spring that list gets whittled down, with the help of expert consultation.

The recommendations are given to the prize-awarding institutions which determine final selections: the Royal Swedish Academy of Sciences confers the prizes for physics, chemistry, and economics; the Karolinska Institute confers the prize for physiology or medicine; the Swedish Academy confers the prize for literature; and the Norwegian Nobel Committee confers the prize for peace. A recipient of a Nobel Prize receives a cash prize, diploma, and gold medal.

Did you know?....

Sir John George Melvin Compton

Sir John George Melvin Compton was a Saint Lucian politician who became the first Prime Minister upon independence in February 1979. He is called the 'Father of the Nation'. He was born April 29, 1925. He died September 7, 2007.

Sir George Frederick Lawrence Charles

Sir George F. L. Charles was a trade unionist, politician, founder of the Saint Lucia Labour Party and Chief Minister of Saint Lucia in the 1960s. George F. L. Charles Airport, in Castries, is named in his honour.

He was born June 7, 1916. He died July 26, 2004.

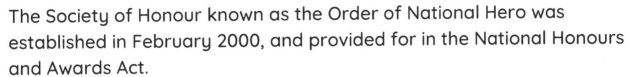

The Society of Honour known as the Order of National Hero was established in February 2000, and provided for in the National Honours and Awards Act.

The Award of National Hero was announced on the occasion of Saint Lucia's 36th Anniversary of Independence on 22 February 2015.

Selection Criteria

The Honour of National Hero is conferred upon any person who was born in Saint Lucia or who at the time of his or her death was a citizen of Saint Lucia and who has -

(a) given outstanding service to Saint Lucia where that service has altered the course of the history of Saint Lucia

(b) given service to Saint Lucia which has been exemplified by visionary and pioneering leadership, extraordinary achievements or attainment of the highest excellence , and which has redounded to the honour of Saint Lucia; or

(c) through his or her heroic exploits or sacrifices contributed to the improvement of the economic and social conditions of Saint Lucia and Saint Lucians generally.

Did you know?...

Dame Pearlette Louisy

Dame Calliopa Pearlette Louisy was the first female appointed Governor General of Saint Lucia. Dame Pearlette Louisy Primary School, in Union, Castries, and the street, Dame Pearlette Louisy Drive, in Laborie, are named in her honour. She was born June 8, 1946.

Ronald 'Boo' Hinkson

Ronald "Boo" Hinkson is a St. Lucian musician who combines jazz with soca music. Boo specialises in playing both the electric and classical guitar.

Dame Marie Selipha 'Sesenne' Descartes

Marie Descartes, a chantwelle and cultural icon, is recognized for her contributions towards Saint Lucia's folk culture. She was called the 'Queen of Culture'. She was born March 28, 1914. She died August 11, 2010.

Levern Spencer

Levern Donaline Spencer is Saint Lucia's first women's high jump athlete to compete in the Olympics. She was born June 23, 1984.
The street, Levern Spencer Drive, in Babonneau, is named in her honour.

Sir Dunstan St.Omer

Sir Dunstan St.Omer is one of Saint Lucia's famous artists. He designed the National Flag of Saint Lucia. He was born October 27, 1927.
He died May 5, 2015.

Daren Sammy

Daren Sammy is Saint Lucia's first cricketer to be captain of the West Indies Cricket Team.
He was born December 20, 1983.
Daren Sammy Cricket Stadium, in Beausejour, is named in his honour.

Websites

https://archive.stlucia.gov.lc/saint_lucia/the_flower_festivals_la_rose_and_la_marguerite.htm

https://www.nobelprize.org/alfred-nobel/

https://www.britannica.com/story/how-do-you-get-a-nobel-prize

http://www.stluciagovernmenthouse.com/history.html

https://www.islandervillas.com/best-villa-travel-guide-in-st-lucia/sulphur-springs-the-worlds-only-drive-in-volcano

https://www.afar.com/places/maria-islands-nature-reserve

https://www.officeholidays.com/holidays/saint-lucia/saint-lucia-independence-day#:~:text=When%20is%20Saint%20Lucia%20Independence,of%20the%20Commonwealth%20of%20Nations.

https://www.britannica.com/place/Saint-Lucia/Independence

http://saintluciaconsulateny.org/about-saint-lucia/saint-lucia-coat-of-arms/

https://www.waymarking.com/waymarks/WMNFZ1_Andrew_Carnegie_Public_Library_Castries_Saint_Lucia

http://www.slupl.edu.lc/2016/02/history.html

https://www.diamondstlucia.com/history

https://stlucia-history.com/wp/sugar/#:~:text=The%20first%20major%20crop%20to,the%20island%20growing%20sugar%20cane.

https://governorgeneral.govt.lc/history-tours

http://www.saintluciavolcanotour.com/volcanohistory.html

Books
"A History of St. Lucia – Jolien Harmsen, Guy Ellis, Robert Devaux"